MAYER SMITH

Crimson Wings and Moonlit Desires

First edition

This book was professionally typeset on Reedsy.
Find out more at reedsy.com

Contents

One

The Moonlit Encounter

Lyra stood on the edge of the cliff, the cold wind tangling her dark hair around her face as she gazed into the abyss below. The moon hung heavy in the sky, its pale light illuminating the jagged rocks and the restless sea that stretched endlessly before her. The sound of the waves crashing against the shore below was hypnotic, a constant rhythm that seemed to echo the pulse in her chest.

There was something eerie about the night—the air was thick with tension, charged with a sense of impending change. Lyra could feel it in the very marrow of her bones, a foreboding she couldn't shake. She had always been drawn to the sea, to the isolation of the cliffs where she could think, breathe, and escape from the weight of her family's expectations. But tonight, something felt different. She could almost sense the eyes upon her, hidden in the shadows.

She wrapped her arms tighter around her body, trying to shake off the uneasy feeling that clung to her. The wind howled through the trees behind her, but she didn't turn to face the familiar path that led back to the mansion. Her feet were rooted to the ground, as if something—or someone—was holding her in place.

And then she heard it.

A soft rustle, a disturbance in the stillness. Lyra's heart skipped a beat as her eyes darted around the cliff's edge, but there was nothing there—nothing but the endless darkness and the silver moon. Yet the sensation of being watched, of being hunted, was growing stronger, more pressing with every passing second.

A shadow moved in the corner of her vision, just beyond the reach of the moonlight. Lyra's breath caught in her throat, and for the first time, she felt the full weight of the curse that had hung over her family for generations. She had spent her life trying to ignore the strange stories, the whispers of darkness that followed her bloodline, but tonight they felt real. Too real.

Before she could even react, a figure emerged from the shadows.

He moved like a predator, silent and fluid, his presence almost ethereal. Lyra's first thought was that he was a ghost, a specter from her past that had come to haunt her. But as he stepped into the moonlight, her heart stuttered in her chest.

The man who stood before her was unlike anyone she had ever seen. His eyes—an unnaturally bright green—glowed in the darkness, piercing her like a blade. His features were sharp, angular, as if carved from stone. Dark hair, wild and unkempt, framed a face that was both beautiful and unsettling. He wore a long, black cloak that billowed in the wind, its edges tattered, as though it had seen centuries of battle.

Lyra's breath caught in her throat. There was something undeniably familiar about him, but she couldn't place it. Her pulse quickened, a sense of dread spiraling in her stomach.

"You shouldn't be here," the man said, his voice low and rasping, as if it had not been used in years. It had a magnetic quality, an almost hypnotic pull that made her knees weak.

Lyra took a step back, unsure whether she should run or face him. "Who are you?" she asked, her voice barely more than a whisper.

The stranger's lips curled into a half-smile, though it didn't reach his eyes. "Does it matter?" he replied. "You've already seen too much."

A shiver ran down Lyra's spine, her instincts screaming at her to flee. But she couldn't—she was rooted to the spot, transfixed by his gaze. There was something dangerous about him, something ancient, and yet… she felt an undeniable pull, a magnetism that lured her closer.

"Why are you here?" she asked, trying to steady her voice. "What do you want from me?"

His smile faltered, his eyes narrowing as if trying to decipher her very soul. "What I want is not the question, Lyra. The question is what you want—and whether or not you're willing to accept the truth."

Lyra froze at the sound of her name. There was something unsettling about the way he spoke it, as if he knew her better than anyone. She hadn't told him her name. She hadn't told anyone where she was going tonight. She looked into his eyes, searching for some sign that he was just a figment of her imagination, but there was nothing there but the cold weight of truth.

"I don't know what you mean," she said, trying to remain calm, though her heart was racing in her chest.

The man took a step forward, closing the distance between them. His presence was overwhelming, his aura dark and heavy. "You're not just anyone, Lyra. You never have been. Your bloodline… it's cursed, just like mine." His voice dropped to a near whisper. "We are bound by something ancient. Something neither of us can escape."

Lyra felt a chill creep down her spine. "What are you talking about?" she demanded, her voice trembling despite her best efforts to remain composed.

His gaze softened for the briefest moment, and then it was gone, replaced by an unreadable mask. "I came to warn you," he said. "There are those who will stop at nothing to keep you from understanding what you are, what you were meant to be. And there are those who will destroy you if you try to break the chains that bind you."

Lyra's mind was racing. Her family had never spoken of curses, of bloodlines, of destinies that could not be altered. They had always kept her sheltered, protected from the world outside. But here, with this stranger before her, she felt the weight of her heritage bearing down on her like never before.

"I don't know what you're talking about," she whispered, shaking her head. "I'm just—"

"Just a pawn in a game you can't even comprehend," he finished for her, his voice sharp. "But you don't have to be. You don't have to follow the path they've laid out for you. You have a choice, Lyra."

Her heart pounded in her chest. "What choice?"

The man stepped closer, so close now that she could feel the heat of his body, even through the chill of the night air. His breath was warm against her skin. "You can accept your fate," he said, his eyes glowing in the moonlight. "Or you can fight it—and in doing so, you will learn the truth about who you really are."

Lyra's breath caught in her throat. The air seemed to thicken around them, charged with the weight of his words. She felt as though her world had just been turned upside down. What truth? What was he trying to tell her?

Before she could ask another question, the man turned sharply, his cloak swirling around him like a storm. "But be careful, Lyra," he said over his shoulder. "The path you choose will not be easy. There will be more shadows, more enemies. And if you aren't careful… you'll lose more than just yourself."

With that, he was gone—vanished into the night as if he had never been there.

Lyra stood frozen, her breath coming in shallow gasps. The wind whipped around her, but the chill that ran through her wasn't from the cold. It was something deeper, something far more unsettling.

She didn't know who he was, or what he wanted, but one thing was certain—her life was about to change forever. And whether she liked it or not, the moon had cast its shadow over her fate.

And there was no turning back now.

Two

Whispers in the Dark

The next few days passed in a blur for Lyra. The world around her seemed to spin slower, the edges of her reality growing sharp and out of focus. She couldn't stop thinking about the man—the stranger who had come out of nowhere, spoken words that had set her mind on fire. She could still feel the intensity of his gaze, the warmth of his breath against her skin, the unshakable sensation that something was coming, something inevitable, like a storm on the horizon.

Her heart would race at odd moments, her mind spiraling back to that encounter, trying to make sense of it, but it made no sense at all. Who was he? Why did he know her name? And why had he looked at her like she was someone—or something—he recognized, someone he had been waiting for?

Her family tried to keep her busy, as they always did. There were dinners to attend, meetings to sit through, and social obligations she could never escape. But nothing felt right anymore. She felt like a marionette, strings pulled tight by forces she couldn't understand, couldn't see.

She spent most of her nights walking the vast grounds of her family estate, seeking solace in the silence of the gardens. The nights had grown colder since that encounter, the air thick with a sense of expectation, the moon hanging high above, watching her every move. Tonight was no different.

Lyra slipped out of the house unnoticed, wrapping herself in a dark shawl. The moonlight bathed everything in an ethereal glow, casting long, haunting shadows that seemed to move and shift with the wind. The gravel path crunched beneath her boots as she made her way toward the edge of the estate, toward the old stone gate that led to the forest. She had no particular destination in mind—only the need to escape, to breathe, to clear her head.

The trees at the edge of the forest whispered in the wind, their leaves rustling like secrets. Lyra paused at the entrance, glancing over her shoulder, half expecting someone to follow her, to stop her from venturing further. But no one was there. The house loomed in the distance, a dark silhouette against the night sky.

For a moment, she considered turning back. But something inside her urged her forward, deeper into the darkness.

She didn't know how far she had walked when the air around her grew heavier, charged with an unseen presence. The breeze died, the world holding its breath. Her skin prickled with awareness, and her pulse quickened as she realized she wasn't alone.

There, standing at the edge of the woods, just beyond the moon's reach, was the man—the stranger from the cliff.

Her heart leaped into her throat as she froze in place, her breath caught in her chest. The man hadn't moved, hadn't even looked at her, but the tension in the air crackled around them. His cloak fluttered faintly, the only sign that he was real, that he was there.

For a long moment, neither of them spoke. The silence stretched between them, thick and oppressive, until finally, his voice broke through, low and steady.

"You're persistent," he said, his tone almost amused. "I warned you to stay away."

Lyra's hands clenched into fists at her sides, a mix of fear and anger boiling inside her. "Why are you following me?" she demanded, though she already knew the answer, or at least part of it. "What do you want from me?"

His lips curled into a faint smile, though his eyes remained unreadable. "I told you before, Lyra. You're not like the others. And there are things you need to know."

Her throat tightened. She wanted to turn and run, to escape the suffocating pull of his presence. But she couldn't. Something in her refused to leave, as if the answers to everything she had ever wondered lay just beyond his reach.

"Stop following me," she said, her voice shakier than she intended. "I don't know who you are, or what you want, but I want nothing to do with this… curse, or whatever you're talking about."

He finally looked at her then, his gaze piercing through the darkness, locking onto hers with an intensity that made her heart skip a beat. "You can't escape it, Lyra. You are already a part of it. The blood in your veins, the history that courses through your family—it's all connected. The curse isn't something you can outrun."

A chill ran through her, despite the warmth of the night. The air seemed to tighten around her, the very earth beneath her feet feeling unstable. She swallowed hard, trying to gather the fragments of her thoughts. "What does that mean? What curse?"

He took a step forward, closing the distance between them, and Lyra instinctively took a step back, her heart pounding. But he didn't stop. He was close now, close enough that she could see the faint glow of his eyes, could smell the wild scent of the forest in his skin.

"The curse is tied to your bloodline, Lyra," he said softly, almost too softly, as though the very words were dangerous. "It's a curse that has been passed down for generations, a darkness that has lingered, waiting for you. And it has always known you would come. That's why you can't avoid it. You are the key."

Lyra's breath caught in her throat. "What do you mean? What does that have to do with me?"

He stepped closer still, his presence overwhelming, filling the space between them. Lyra could feel the heat radiating off him, the tension in the air thick with unspoken truths. "You are part of something much larger than you realize," he said. "You have the power to break it—or to fall victim to it, just like the rest of your family."

She opened her mouth to argue, to deny it all, but the words stuck in her throat. There was something in his eyes, something that made her believe, even if she didn't want to. She felt it in the pit of her stomach, a rising sense of inevitability. The pieces of the puzzle she had been trying to ignore were beginning to fall into place.

A faint noise behind her—a twig snapping, the sound of a footstep in the forest—made her turn her head sharply. She saw nothing, but the sensation of being watched crept up her spine like ice.

The man's eyes darkened, and he placed a hand on her arm, his grip firm but not unkind. "Don't look away, Lyra," he warned, his voice suddenly cold. "There are things in the dark that you don't understand. And they're closing in on you."

Lyra looked up at him, her pulse racing. She wanted to pull away from him, to run back to the safety of the house, to her old life where things made sense. But deep down, she knew that wasn't possible anymore. The man was right. The curse was already there, in the shadows, watching her.

"What do I do?" she asked, the question slipping from her lips before she could stop herself.

The man stared at her, his eyes unreadable, and for a moment, Lyra could have sworn she saw something in them—something soft, something painful.

"You have to choose, Lyra," he said quietly, his voice low and almost regretful. "And when you do, everything will change."

His words hung in the air between them, a promise and a warning wrapped in one. Before Lyra could respond, before she could even begin to comprehend the magnitude of what he was saying, the man turned and melted into the darkness, disappearing as quickly as he had come.

She stood there, heart pounding, breath coming in shallow gasps, staring into the empty night. The silence around her was deafening. The world felt different now, as though the very ground beneath her feet had shifted.

But there was no turning back now. The curse, the truth—it was all coming for her. And whatever choice she made, she knew one thing for certain: nothing would ever be the same again.

Three

The Secrets Between Us

Lyra's heart hammered in her chest as she made her way back to the mansion, the night air cold against her skin. Her mind raced with fragments of what had just happened, the encounter with the stranger still vivid in her memory. His words had dug into her like thorns, each one a reminder that her life was no longer her own, that it had never been. The curse, the bloodline, the darkness following her—it all felt like a trap, and yet she couldn't escape it. She didn't know if she wanted to.

The trees on the edge of the estate loomed like silent sentinels, their twisted branches reaching for the sky as if trying to grasp her in their cold, skeletal embrace. The faint scent of damp earth and pine lingered in the air, but it did nothing to calm the restlessness in her soul. Every step she took felt heavier, the weight of his words pressing down on her. She couldn't ignore the way her thoughts had been consumed by him, his presence, his warnings.

And yet, even as the fear wrapped itself around her, there was something else—a longing, a pull that she couldn't quite explain. When he had looked at her, when he had spoken her name, something inside her had stirred, a flicker of recognition deep within her bones. As if she had always known him, as if she had always been waiting for him.

The moon hung high above, casting long, slanted shadows across the stone path leading back to the mansion. Her footsteps echoed, a hollow sound in the night, and for a moment, she thought she heard something else, something following her. But when she glanced over her shoulder, there was nothing there—nothing but the ever-present darkness, creeping and shifting with the wind.

She quickened her pace, eager to get inside, to lose herself in the safety of her home. Yet, as she neared the door, she saw him again.

Caden.

He stood at the top of the stairs leading to the mansion's grand entrance, his silhouette framed by the flickering light from the hallway behind him. He was watching her, his dark eyes unreadable, his posture tense, as though he had been waiting for her. Lyra's pulse stuttered at the sight of him—his presence, as always, unnerving, yet magnetic.

"I thought you might return," he said, his voice low, barely a whisper, but the words carried a weight to them. His gaze flickered over her, his eyes narrowing slightly, as though searching for something. "You didn't answer your doorbell."

Lyra stopped at the bottom of the stairs, her throat dry. Her gaze flickered to the ground, avoiding his steady stare. "I—"

"Don't bother with the excuses," he interrupted, his voice sharper now, more insistent. "I've been watching you, Lyra. I know what you've been doing."

She felt a flash of panic rush through her. "Watching me? You've been—"

"I'm not the only one," he said, his voice tinged with something almost… resigned. "You're not as alone in this as you think."

The words hit her like a slap, and her heart began to race again, faster this time, her stomach twisting. "What do you mean?" She couldn't help the sharpness in her tone, the bite of desperation creeping into her voice. "What's going on? Who else has been watching me?"

He stepped down the stairs slowly, his movements deliberate, fluid, almost predatory. The air around them thickened, crackling with tension. She felt a tightness in her chest, as if the very atmosphere was pushing in on her.

"It's not just me," Caden said, his voice softer now, but no less dangerous. "There are others—people who know what you are, who know who you are."

Lyra's breath caught in her throat, her pulse quickening again. "What do you mean, what I am?"

Caden hesitated, his gaze flickering for a moment, almost as if he were deciding whether to continue. But when he looked back at her, his eyes were unyielding, as if this was something he couldn't avoid any longer.

"You don't know everything about yourself, do you, Lyra?" His voice was low, each word deliberate. "The power you've inherited—your bloodline isn't just cursed, it's part of something much bigger. And you've been running from it your whole life."

She shook her head, trying to make sense of his words, but it was as if they were a jigsaw puzzle with too many missing pieces. "I don't understand. What am I supposed to do with all of this?"

Caden stepped closer, his presence overwhelming, and Lyra instinctively took a step back, her breath shallow. He seemed to notice the distance she put between them, but he didn't stop. His gaze softened ever so slightly, as if he was holding back something, something that wasn't meant for her to know just yet.

"You can't run from this forever," he said quietly. "You've already started to feel it, haven't you? The pull. The pull of something that's been with you since you were born. It's been in your veins, Lyra, all along."

Her throat constricted, the air around them feeling too tight, too suffocating. The wind had stopped, leaving a heavy silence that seemed to press in on them from all sides. She had heard stories, vague whispers in her childhood about her family's legacy, but never anything concrete. There had always been shadows in the corners of her life, but no one had ever been able to explain them.

And now, Caden was standing in front of her, telling her things she didn't want to hear, things that felt too real.

"I don't want this," she whispered, barely hearing her own words. "I just want to be normal. I don't want to be part of whatever this is."

Caden reached out, his fingers brushing against her arm. His touch was warm, steady, and Lyra felt a jolt of something unexpected shoot through her—a spark of connection that made her feel both grounded and unmoored at once.

"I know you don't," he murmured, his eyes softening, his voice gentler now, though still filled with an unspoken tension. "But you don't have a choice. None of us do. The curse binds us all. But it's not just a curse—it's a legacy. And you have to decide if you're going to embrace it or let it destroy you."

Her head swam with the weight of his words, each one pressing deeper, pushing her toward something she wasn't ready for. She opened her mouth to respond, but before she could speak, a sudden noise from inside the mansion interrupted them. A door creaked open, the sound sharp in the quiet of the night.

Lyra turned quickly, her heart still racing, her mind spinning. Someone had heard them.

"Go inside," Caden said, his voice low and commanding, but there was an urgency to it now, an edge that made her pause. "We'll talk later."

Before she could protest, he had already turned and melted into the shadows, disappearing as suddenly as he had arrived. Lyra stood there for a long moment, her heart thumping in her chest, staring at the empty space where he had been.

The sound of footsteps approaching from inside the house grew louder, and she quickly turned to head back to the door. She didn't look back.

But as she stepped inside, she couldn't shake the feeling that things had shifted, that her life was no longer her own, that the shadows were closing in. And no matter how hard she tried, there was no escaping the pull of whatever fate awaited her.

Four

The Betrayal

T he grand halls of the mansion were silent in the early hours of the morning. Lyra could feel the weight of the darkness pressing against the high ceilings, the opulent chandeliers casting faint shadows on the polished marble floors. The silence seeped into her bones and deep into her skin, and it unsettled her more than the sound of her own racing heartbeat.

She had spent hours walking the halls, pacing, trying to make sense of the whirlwind of revelations that had stormed her life. Caden's cryptic words still rang in her ears. He had told her things she wasn't ready to hear, things that would forever alter her path. The curse, bloodline, and legacy were too much for her to grasp. But the strange, undeniable pull she had felt whenever he was near—when he had touched her—was something she couldn't shake. And neither could the burning questions that gnawed at her, relentless, consuming.

She had been avoiding the study all evening. The study was where her father worked late into the night, where the weight of their family's secrets was locked away in dusty old books behind closed doors. It was the last place she wanted to be, but she knew she couldn't avoid it forever. She had to face the truth, whatever it was.

When she finally stepped inside, the study was dimly lit, the heavy curtains drawn tight against the early morning light. The scent of aged leather and ink filled the air, mingling with the faint tang of tobacco smoke from the pipe her father often smoked in the late hours. She could see the faint outline of his figure at the desk, the low glow of a lamp casting his face in sharp contrast.

Her father, a man who had always been the pillar of her world, had begun to change in ways she couldn't explain. He had always been distant, but lately, there was something colder in his eyes, something more guarded. It was as if the man she had known for her entire life was slowly slipping away, replaced by someone she couldn't recognize. And the more she thought about it, the more she realized it wasn't just him. There was a strange air of secrecy around her entire family—a tension that she could feel in her bones but couldn't place.

"Father," she said softly, her voice tentative as she approached the desk. He looked up slowly, his expression unreadable. His eyes, dark like hers, seemed to shimmer with a quiet intensity she had never seen before.

"Lyra," he said, his voice calm, yet there was an undercurrent of something else in it—something she couldn't quite place. He motioned for her to sit, but she remained standing. Her instincts were on high alert, and she couldn't shake the feeling that she was walking into something she wasn't ready for.

"I've been thinking about what you said," she began, taking a deep breath. "About the curse. About our bloodline."

Her father's expression didn't change, but there was a flicker of something—something almost imperceptible—that passed over his face. "You've been listening to Caden, haven't you?" His voice was steady, but Lyra could hear the sharpness beneath the surface.

She hesitated. Caden's name had slipped out before she could stop it, and her father's reaction confirmed everything she had feared. There was more to the man than she had realized, and not all of it was good. "He said I need to know the truth, that it's my destiny," she continued, her voice faltering slightly. "He said that I have no choice, that the curse will consume me if I don't embrace it. What does he mean? What do you know about this?"

Her father's eyes darkened, and for the first time, she saw a flicker of something like fear behind them. It was gone almost as quickly as it had appeared, but the damage had been done. Her heart tightened in her chest, and the air seemed to grow colder, heavier.

"Lyra," he said softly, almost too gently. "There are things you don't understand. Things you're not ready to understand.

Caden doesn't know everything. And neither do you."

Her pulse quickened. She could feel her world beginning to crack, the seams of the life she had always known beginning to split open. "What do you mean? What aren't you telling me?"

Her father rose from his chair, the sudden movement startling her. His eyes locked onto hers, and she saw the raw edge of something darker in his gaze—something dangerous, something she had never seen in him before. "You need to forget about Caden," he said, his voice low and urgent. "He's not who he seems to be. He's playing a game, and you're nothing more than a pawn in it."

Her heart pounded in her chest. "What are you talking about?" She stepped back instinctively, her mind reeling. "You can't just tell me to forget him. He's the only one who's been honest with me."

Her father's expression tightened. "He's dangerous, Lyra. You have no idea what he's involved in. And if you get too close to him, you'll bring ruin to yourself and everything we've worked for. I won't let that happen."

She swallowed hard, the weight of his words settling over her like a cloak of ice. "Why?" she asked, her voice trembling. "What does he want from me? What is all of this about?"

Her father's face hardened, and he took a step toward her, his hands clenched at his sides. "What I want is for you to stay away from him. Caden is not your ally. He's not your friend.

He's part of the very darkness that has plagued our family for generations. And if you continue down this path, you will regret it."

The room seemed to close in around her, the walls pressing in on her with every word. Her father's anger, his fear, the weight of his warnings—everything about this moment felt wrong. Her mind raced, desperately trying to piece together the truth, but there were too many pieces missing, too many things she didn't know.

And then, as if on cue, a soft knock came at the door.

Lyra's breath caught in her throat. The timing couldn't have been worse.

"Father?" a voice called from outside. Lyra's heart skipped. It was one of the servants, her voice anxious. "There's someone here to see you. A man."

Her father's face darkened further, and for a moment, Lyra saw something flicker in his eyes—something that might have been guilt, or fear, or both. He turned away from her without another word, moving quickly toward the door.

But as he opened it, a tall figure stepped inside, his silhouette framed by the dim light from the hallway. Lyra's pulse stilled as she saw who it was.

Caden.

He stepped into the study, his eyes locking onto hers with that familiar intensity. Her heart skipped, the tension between them palpable, but her father's presence seemed to crush the air between them.

"Caden," her father said, his voice colder than she had ever heard it. "What are you doing here?"

Caden's lips curled into a smile, but it didn't reach his eyes. His gaze flicked to Lyra before settling back on her father. "I came to speak with you," he said, his voice smooth and even, but with an edge of something else—something she couldn't quite place. "I think it's time we finally talk about the past."

Lyra's breath caught in her throat. The tension in the room was suffocating, and the room seemed to spin around her as she realized that the lies, the secrets, were finally unraveling.

And she was right in the middle of it all.

Five

The Dangers of Desire

The heavy scent of jasmine filled the air, mingling with the lingering musk of the early evening fog. Lyra ambled through the garden, the soft rustling of leaves underfoot the only sound that accompanied her thoughts. The estate, sprawling and grand, seemed to breathe with her, the ancient trees standing tall and silent as though watching over her every move. It had always been her sanctuary, a place of calm amidst the chaos of her life, but tonight, the beauty of the garden felt foreign, as though the world she had once known was slipping away with every step she took.

Caden's words echoed in her mind, their weight heavier than the moonlit sky above. "You can't run from this forever." The curse. Her bloodline. Her destiny. She had tried to push the thoughts away, tried to bury the terror rising in her chest, but they clung to her like an unshakable shadow. She had never felt so exposed, so vulnerable, her very identity torn open before her.

The touch of his hand, warm and sure, lingered on her skin, and she fought to suppress the shiver that crawled up her spine. There was something about Caden, something dangerous, magnetic, that drew her to him against her will. The kiss they had shared—the brief, heated brush of lips—had stirred something deep inside her, a yearning she couldn't explain. He was a mystery, wrapped in shadows, and though part of her feared him, another part was consumed by the desire to unravel him, to uncover the secrets he held.

But that kiss… it was a mistake, wasn't it?

The garden seemed to close in around her as the evening air thickened, her breath coming faster with each passing second. She had never been one to succumb to the reckless pull of desire, not like this. But Caden—Caden had a way of making her forget herself, of making her forget the world and its rules, and for that brief moment, she had felt as if she could burn away her past, her fears, and embrace whatever future he was offering.

The sound of footsteps behind her made her freeze.

"Lyra," Caden's voice drifted through the night like a whisper on the wind. It was soft, but his presence was unmistakable, pressing into her skin like the weight of the moon itself. She didn't turn around, didn't have to. She knew he was there.

She didn't answer, not immediately. The words she wanted to

say tangled in her throat, thick and suffocating, but nothing came. It was as if she had been rendered mute, paralyzed by the tension that seemed to stretch between them like a taut wire, ready to snap.

He took another step closer, the ground beneath his boots barely making a sound. The heat of his body seemed to reach her even though they stood apart, and she felt that same pull she couldn't ignore. It was magnetic, impossible to fight.

Finally, she turned to face him.

Caden stood a few feet away, his dark eyes glittering in the soft light of the garden, watching her with a mixture of intent and something she couldn't place—something raw and unspoken. His mouth curled into a small, almost amused smile, but there was an edge to it that made her heart skip a beat.

"Why are you following me?" Lyra asked, her voice more breathless than she intended, the words tumbling out before she could stop them. The question was half accusation, half plea, and it betrayed her uncertainty.

Caden didn't move, his gaze unwavering as he regarded her with a mix of admiration and something darker, something more dangerous. His eyes softened for a moment, and he took a step closer, the space between them narrowing with each breath.

"I'm not following you, Lyra," he said, his voice low, almost soothing. "I'm here because you need me. Whether you want to admit it or not."

The words hit her like a cold splash of water, and she took an instinctive step back, her pulse quickening. "Need you?" she repeated, a bitter laugh bubbling in her chest. "I don't need anyone, especially not someone like you."

His eyes flashed, a storm of emotions swirling beneath the surface. But before she could react, he stepped forward again, closing the distance between them so that they were standing toe to toe, so close that she could feel the heat of his body, smell the faint scent of tobacco and the forest in his clothes.

"You don't have to admit it now," he murmured, his voice growing hushed, almost intimate. "But you will. You'll realize that you need me when everything around you begins to fall apart. When you see the truth for what it really is. And when you realize that you can't escape what you are."

The words wrapped around her, sinking into her skin like thorns, twisting inside her until she could barely breathe. The tension between them was suffocating, the space between them charged with something she couldn't name, but the feeling of his presence was overwhelming. The dangerous heat of him pressed against her, and she couldn't help but wonder if he was right—if there was something about him she couldn't escape, something that would pull her under no matter how much she fought.

"I don't know what you want from me," she said, her voice trembling despite her best efforts to remain strong. She was trying to resist, to push him away, but part of her—a deep, unspoken part of her—wanted him to come closer. "But I don't want to be part of whatever this is."

His gaze softened, his eyes studying her face as though he was memorizing every detail. "What is it that you want, Lyra?" His voice was barely a whisper now, so close she could feel the words against her skin. "Do you want to keep pretending that this—" He gestured between them, the space between them crackling with energy. "—doesn't mean anything? That you don't feel the pull, the connection?"

Her breath hitched, her chest tightening as her heart pounded wildly in her ears. No, she wanted to say. This isn't real. This can't be real. But the truth was, she did feel it. She felt it every time he was near, every time he spoke to her, his voice a thread woven into the very fabric of her soul.

She opened her mouth to protest, but the words died on her lips. Instead, she found herself taking another step toward him, against her will, her breath shallow as she moved into the heat of his presence. His hands, warm and sure, came up to her face, cupping her chin gently, tilting her head back so she had no choice but to look into his eyes.

And then he kissed her.

The world tilted on its axis. Every thought, every fear, every fragment of doubt shattered like glass. The kiss was soft at first, testing, teasing, and Lyra's body responded before her mind could catch up. She felt herself falling into it, into him, into the promise of something forbidden, something dangerous. His lips were warm and urgent, coaxing, pulling her deeper into the storm that was him.

But it wasn't just the kiss. It was the way he held her, the way he made her feel as though they were the only two people in the world. It was the way his touch seemed to melt the walls she had built around her heart, the way his breath mingled with hers, as though they were already one.

When they finally pulled apart, the distance between them felt unbearable. Lyra's chest was heaving, her breath shallow, as though the kiss had stolen the air from her lungs. Caden's face was close, his lips just inches from hers, his eyes dark with desire and something more—something she couldn't name.

"You don't have to fight it, Lyra," he said, his voice husky, his hand still resting on her cheek. "It's already inside you. You can feel it. The truth. The connection. We're bound together whether you like it or not."

She wanted to push him away, to deny it, but the truth of his words settled over her like a weight, and the feeling of his touch burned through her, making it impossible to escape.

Her heart was racing, her body alive with something she couldn't name. Desire. Fear. Both. And it scared her, more than anything else.

"I don't want this," she whispered, though the words felt hollow, like a lie.

But Caden only smiled, his lips curling slightly as he pulled her closer. "It's already begun, Lyra," he murmured, his lips brushing against her ear. "And you can't stop it."

As the moon bathed them in its light, Lyra realized, with a sudden, sharp clarity, that she was no longer in control. And she wasn't sure if she ever had been.

Six

Tides of Fate

The morning sky hung heavy with clouds, a wash of gray that threatened to spill over the horizon at any moment. Lyra stood by the window, her hands pressed against the cool glass as she gazed out at the sea. The waves were choppy, battering against the jagged rocks below, but the beauty of the view was lost on her. Her mind was a storm of its own, chaotic, frantic, and full of questions that refused to be answered.

Caden's face, his eyes burning with intensity, was all she could see. You are part of something much larger than you realize. His words echoed in her mind, rippling through her thoughts like the crashing waves outside. The pull, he had said. The connection. The truth about her bloodline, about the curse that ran through her veins. It all seemed too much to take in, too impossible to understand.

She had tried to ignore the connection between them, tried to push away the undeniable magnetism that had drawn her to him. But every time she saw him, every time he touched her, the walls she had so carefully constructed around herself began to crumble.

Her pulse quickened as she thought of the kiss they had shared in the garden, the way his lips had ignited something within her—a fire she couldn't extinguish, a desire that had burned through the fog of her confusion. And yet, as much as she longed for him, there was a part of her that knew he was dangerous, that he was wrapped in shadows, a man whose true intentions were still a mystery.

Her reflection in the window was pale, her face drawn and tired, as though the weight of the secrets she had learned had already begun to take their toll on her. But she couldn't run from this— not anymore. She had tried to, tried to bury the truth beneath layers of denial, but it was all beginning to surface. The pull, the curse, the legacy. It was all connected, and she was the key.

A soft knock on the door interrupted her thoughts, and she turned quickly, her heart skipping a beat. She had been avoiding the servants, avoiding her family, avoiding everyone who might ask about the storm that was swirling inside her. But now, she had no choice but to face whatever was coming.

"Miss Lyra," came the voice from the other side, tentative but firm. "Your father wishes to speak with you."

Her stomach tightened. She hadn't seen her father since their last conversation in the study, and the tension between them had only grown since then. He had warned her to stay away from Caden, but the more she thought about it, the more she realized that there was something her father wasn't telling her. There were things she needed to understand—about Caden, about the curse, about everything—and her father was the only one who could provide the answers.

"I'll be down in a moment," she replied, her voice steady despite the flutter of anxiety in her chest.

The minutes felt like hours as she prepared herself to face her father. The weight of his disapproval, of his secrecy, hung heavily on her. But there was a part of her that was desperate to know the truth, desperate to understand why her life had been turned upside down.

She descended the grand staircase slowly, her footsteps echoing through the empty hall. The house was silent, its grandeur almost oppressive in its stillness. The air was thick with the scent of wood and dust, and the low hum of the fireplace in the parlor provided the only warmth in the otherwise cold room.

Her father sat at his desk in the study, a flicker of movement as he glanced up from the papers in front of him. His expression was as impassive as ever, but Lyra could see the tension in his shoulders, the way his jaw clenched when he noticed her approaching.

"Lyra," he said, his voice tight with something she couldn't name. "Sit down."

She did as he asked, taking a seat across from him at the grand oak desk. The silence stretched between them, thick and uncomfortable, until her father finally broke it with a sigh.

"I know what you've been doing," he said, his voice low, almost too quiet. "I know you've been seeing him."

Lyra's breath caught in her throat, and she felt a flash of heat rush to her cheeks. She had hoped her father didn't know, hoped she could keep her growing connection with Caden a secret for just a little while longer. But it was useless. There was no hiding from the truth now.

"You've been warned, Lyra," her father continued, his eyes narrowing as he watched her. "Caden is not someone you can trust. He's playing a game, and you're nothing more than a pawn in it."

Her heart began to race, the panic rising in her chest like a tide, threatening to overwhelm her. She had never seen her father like this, never seen him so consumed by fear. There was something in his eyes, something dark, that made her question everything she had ever known about him.

"You don't understand," she whispered, her voice trembling. "There's something about him, Father. Something I can't ignore. He's not like the others. He's… different."

Her father's face hardened, his expression cold. "You think I don't know that? You think I don't see the way he looks at you, the way he's been manipulating you? He's dangerous, Lyra. And

I won't let you fall under his spell."

The words stung, but Lyra couldn't deny the truth in them. Caden was dangerous, she knew that. But he was also something else—a mystery, a force she couldn't control, but one that had become inextricably tied to her. The pull between them was undeniable, and no matter how much she tried to push it away, she couldn't escape it.

"I'm not a child anymore," she said, her voice gaining strength as she leaned forward. "I need to know the truth, Father. What is this curse? What does it mean? What's happened to our family?"

Her father's face twisted, a brief flash of pain crossing his features before it was replaced by a mask of resolve. He stood up suddenly, walking over to the fireplace and staring into the flames. The flickering light danced across his face, casting shadows that seemed to deepen the lines in his expression.

"Lyra," he said, his voice low, almost regretful. "I never wanted you to get involved in this. But it's too late now. The curse is tied to our bloodline. It's been passed down through generations, a legacy we can never escape. And Caden…" He turned to look at her then, his gaze hard. "Caden is part of that legacy. He's not just a stranger, not just some fool with dangerous ideas. He's a key to everything."

Lyra's heart skipped a beat as the words sank in. "A key to what?" she asked, her voice barely a whisper.

Her father looked away, his gaze drifting back to the flames. "A key to breaking the curse. Or a key to destroying us all."

The air in the room felt colder suddenly, as though the very walls were closing in on her. She wanted to say something, to ask more questions, but the weight of her father's words held her in place. The room was thick with tension, and every word seemed to carry a heavy price.

"Do you understand now?" her father said, his voice rough with emotion. "Caden is not your ally. He's not someone you can trust. And if you're not careful, he'll lead you down a path that you'll never be able to come back from."

Lyra swallowed hard, the knot in her stomach tightening. She didn't know what to believe anymore, didn't know who to trust. But one thing was clear—her life was spiraling out of her control, and the tide of fate was pulling her deeper into something she couldn't escape.

Seven

The Heart's Dilemma

Lyra's breath caught in her throat as she stepped out onto the balcony, the cold wind whipping through her hair and carrying with it the scent of rain that hadn't quite arrived. The air felt electric, charged with something she couldn't name—a tension that had been building for days, growing with each passing moment. She leaned against the stone railing, her fingers gripping the cool surface as she stared out at the sea, its dark waters churning beneath the storm-heavy sky. It felt like the world was on the brink of something, something that might tear everything apart.

She hadn't slept in days. The visions of Caden—his dark eyes, the heat of his touch, the whisper of his words in her ear—kept her awake, a constant presence in her mind, haunting her even in the quietest moments. The kiss they had shared in the garden had only deepened the confusion in her heart. It had felt like a collision of everything she had ever wanted and everything she had been warned to avoid. The pull between them was undeniable, and it was tearing her apart.

Her father's warnings echoed in her mind, as cold and sharp as the storm clouds gathering above. Caden is not your ally. He is the key to destroying us all. But even as she tried to hold onto his words, the weight of them pressing against her chest, she couldn't push Caden away. She couldn't deny the fire that had sparked between them, a fire that had burned through the haze of her fear and doubt.

She closed her eyes, trying to clear her thoughts, but every time she did, she saw him again—his face, so close to hers, his lips brushing against her skin as he whispered words she couldn't understand, words that had left a mark on her soul. You don't have to fight this, Lyra. She shuddered at the memory, as though his breath still lingered against her skin, the ghost of his touch sending a ripple of longing through her body.

The sound of footsteps behind her brought her back to the present, and she straightened, wiping away the unsettling feeling that had settled over her. She didn't need to turn around to know who it was. The presence was unmistakable, a weight in the air that seemed to draw the world closer, more intense, more immediate.

"Lyra," Caden's voice was low, barely above a whisper, but it cut through the tension like a blade. "You've been avoiding me."

She didn't answer, not at first. Her heart hammered in her

chest, and for a moment, she simply stood there, her back to him, the wind pulling at her hair as if trying to push her into the storm. He was right. She had been avoiding him. Ever since their last encounter, the kiss that had blurred the lines between them, she had tried to keep her distance, tried to focus on something—anything—that wasn't him.

But the truth was, she couldn't. She couldn't escape the pull. The way he made her feel, as if every part of her was awakened, was alive in ways she had never known before. And yet, the fear still lingered—the fear that she was falling into something she couldn't control, something that would destroy her if she wasn't careful.

"You should leave," Lyra said, her voice barely audible above the rising wind, but the words tasted bitter in her mouth, like a plea and a command all at once. "I'm not ready for this. I'm not ready for whatever this is."

Caden's silence was almost more deafening than his words had been. She could feel him behind her, standing too close, the space between them filled with something electric, something alive. It was as though he was waiting, waiting for her to turn, to face him, to see him for what he truly was. But she couldn't. Not yet.

"You're not ready for this?" His voice was laced with an un-readable emotion, something between amusement and regret. "Lyra, you've always known. You've always known this was coming."

She turned then, her breath catching as she faced him. His dark eyes were fixed on her with an intensity that made her knees feel weak, as though he could see straight through her, straight to the very core of who she was. His gaze was hot, but it was also a challenge—a test she wasn't sure she was ready for.

"I don't know what you mean," she said, her voice trembling despite her efforts to hold onto control. "I don't know who you are anymore, Caden."

He stepped closer, and Lyra's breath hitched. The space between them seemed to shrink, the air thick with the weight of unspoken words. The scent of his cologne mixed with the salt of the sea, and it was too much, too overwhelming. She felt the pull again, that magnetic force that made it impossible to take a step back, impossible to look away from him.

"I'm exactly who you think I am," Caden said softly, his voice low and full of something she couldn't place. "But I'm also more than that. More than just the stranger you're afraid of."

Lyra wanted to pull away, wanted to take a step back, but her feet were rooted to the ground. She couldn't look away from him, couldn't move even if she wanted to. The weight of his gaze held her captive, as if his very presence had wrapped around her like a chain, tightening with every breath she took.

"I'm not afraid of you," she whispered, though the words felt like a lie. She was terrified. Terrified of what he could do to her, terrified of what this thing between them was becoming.

Caden's lips quirked into a half-smile, and for a moment, the intensity of his gaze softened, though the air around them was still thick with tension. He reached out then, his fingers brushing against her cheek, a touch that was both gentle and insistent, as though he were tracing the very lines of her soul.

"You should be," he said softly, his voice carrying a note of something dark, something dangerous. "Because this is just the beginning, Lyra. You can't stop it. You can't deny it."

His hand lingered against her cheek, and her pulse quickened, her body betraying her, responding to him in ways she couldn't understand. She wanted to pull away, to push him out of her mind, but her heart was already lost, already tangled in the web he had woven around her.

"Why are you doing this to me?" she asked, her voice breaking with the weight of her own vulnerability. "Why can't you just leave me alone?"

Caden's gaze softened again, and for a brief moment, she saw something in his eyes—something that wasn't just dark and dangerous, but something deeper, something raw, something that made her heart ache. "I can't leave you alone, Lyra," he whispered. "Not now. Not after everything we've shared. Not after what's coming for us."

She shook her head, the confusion in her chest rising like a wave, threatening to drown her. "What's coming for us? What do you mean? What is this? What is happening to me?"

Caden's expression darkened again, his jaw tightening as if the weight of his words was too much to bear. "You're not just caught in this, Lyra. You're the heart of it. The curse is tied to you in ways you can't begin to understand. You're the key to everything. And whether you like it or not, you're already involved."

The words slammed into her like a physical blow, and her knees threatened to give out beneath her. The pull—the truth about her bloodline, the connection to Caden—it all came crashing down on her in an instant. She wanted to run, wanted to escape the suffocating weight of it all, but there was no way out. Not now. Not anymore.

"You need to decide, Lyra," Caden said, his voice a low growl. "You need to decide if you're going to embrace this, embrace us, or if you're going to let it destroy you."

The storm overhead broke then, the first drops of rain falling in a torrent, soaking them both within seconds. Lyra didn't move, didn't speak, her gaze locked onto Caden's as the rain pelted down around them, mingling with the salt of the sea. She was drowning in the storm of emotions inside her, the storm of the world they had awakened together.

She had no choice, no escape.

And deep down, she knew it was already too late.

Eight

The Moon's Reckoning

The moon hung heavy in the sky, its silvery light casting a pale glow over the estate as Lyra made her way through the darkened corridors of the mansion. The air felt thick with anticipation, as if the night itself was holding its breath. Each step she took echoed in the silence, the soft creak of the floorboards beneath her feet the only sound that dared to break the stillness.

She had spent hours wandering the halls, trying to lose herself in the labyrinth of rooms, in the rich tapestries and dark wood of the estate. But it was useless. Her thoughts kept circling back to Caden—the way his touch had branded her skin, the way his words had twisted through her, unraveling the very fabric of everything she thought she knew about herself. You're the key, he had said. You can break the curse, or you can fall victim to it. But what did it mean? What did he mean? And why did the weight of his words feel like a heavy stone in her chest?

She stopped in front of the grand mirror that lined the hallway, its surface reflecting back her weary face, pale and haunted, the dark circles beneath her eyes a stark reminder of how little sleep she had gotten since her encounter with Caden. The person she saw staring back at her seemed foreign, like a shadow of the girl she once was, her identity shifting with each passing moment. The curse, the bloodline, the dark pull of Caden—everything was changing, and Lyra wasn't sure she was ready to face whatever it was that was coming for her.

The soft flicker of a candle caught her eye from the end of the hallway, casting dancing shadows on the walls. It was a faint light, a fragile glow, and for a moment, she wondered if it was simply her imagination playing tricks on her. But no, it was real. Someone was there.

Her heart skipped a beat as she hesitated, her hand lingering on the ornate railing as she stepped forward, drawn to the flickering light like a moth to a flame. Each step she took brought the warmth of the candlelight closer, and as she rounded the corner, she found herself standing in front of the library—her father's sanctuary, the place he retreated to when he wanted to escape the world.

The door was slightly ajar, the faint glow of the candle spilling out from within. Lyra's breath caught in her throat as she took a step forward, her heart pounding in her chest. She hadn't expected to find him here—not tonight, not after their last conversation. He had been so adamant, so cold, his warnings lingering in the air between them like smoke. Stay away from Caden. But she couldn't. No matter how hard she tried, the pull toward him was stronger than ever.

She gently pushed open the door, the hinges creaking as it swung wide, revealing her father sitting at his desk, his back to her. His posture was tense, as though he could sense her presence even before she made herself known. The faint light of the candle flickered against his face, casting sharp shadows across the lines of his expression. He looked different—harder, older. There was something about him tonight, something that made her blood run cold.

"Lyra," he said, his voice low, his tone cutting through the silence like a blade. "You shouldn't be here."

His words felt like a command, an order, but Lyra couldn't turn away. She stepped forward into the room, the weight of her father's gaze heavy on her as she took a seat across from him at the desk. The candlelight between them flickered again, the shadows playing tricks on the walls. The air was thick with tension, and for the first time in her life, Lyra wondered if she was seeing her father for who he truly was.

"I need answers, Father," she said, her voice trembling despite her best efforts to keep it steady. "I need to know what's happening. Why did you tell me to stay away from Caden? What is this curse? What's the truth?"

Her father's gaze flickered briefly, but his expression remained cold, unreadable. He didn't answer immediately, instead turning his attention to the papers scattered across his desk. The flickering candlelight caught the edges of the pages, and for a moment, Lyra thought she saw something there—something hidden beneath the surface, something he was trying to keep from her.

"You think you can just walk into this, Lyra," he said after a long pause, his voice sharp, though there was a trace of weariness in it. "You think you can simply ask questions and expect to understand what's happening. But you don't. You won't. And you'll regret it if you push any further."

She leaned forward, her hands gripping the edge of the desk as she fought to keep her composure. "I have to know," she whispered, her voice almost pleading. "You're not telling me everything. You've kept me in the dark for so long. I deserve to know the truth."

Her father finally looked up at her, his eyes hard and cold, a dark storm brewing behind them. "The truth, Lyra?" he said, his voice low, filled with a coldness that sent a shiver down her spine. "You don't want to know the truth. The truth is more than you can bear. It's a weight you will never be able to carry."

Lyra's breath caught in her throat, her pulse racing as the words hit her like a punch to the gut. She had never seen her father like this—never seen him so broken, so raw. She had always thought of him as untouchable, unshakable. But now, she saw something different in him—a man trapped by something he couldn't control, something that had shaped his life in ways she didn't understand.

"I don't care what it costs," she said, her voice trembling but resolute. "I need to know. Please. I need to understand."

For a moment, her father was silent, his gaze flicking to the window, to the moonlight spilling through the glass. He seemed lost in his thoughts, as though struggling with a decision he had already made long ago. The candlelight flickered again, and for the briefest of moments, Lyra saw something shift in his eyes—a flicker of regret, of fear.

"It's not just a curse, Lyra," he said finally, his voice barely above a whisper. "It's a bloodline. A legacy we can never escape. Our family is bound to something ancient, something dark. The curse was never meant to be broken. It was meant to be controlled."

Lyra felt her heart stop as the weight of his words settled over her. "Controlled?" she repeated, her voice barely a whisper. "What do you mean?"

Her father stood then, his movements stiff, as though the weight of his own words was too much for him to bear. He walked to the window, looking out into the night as the first drops of rain began to fall against the glass. The world outside seemed to darken with every passing moment, as if the storm was rising, pulling them all into something deeper, something darker.

"You are the key, Lyra," he said quietly, his voice filled with something like despair. "But you're not just the key to breaking the curse. You're the key to controlling it. To keeping it from consuming us all."

Lyra's breath hitched as she struggled to process his words. "But I don't understand," she whispered. "How can I control it? How can I be the key?"

Her father turned then, his eyes dark and filled with an unreadable sorrow. "That's what Caden wants you to understand. He's been trying to manipulate you into believing that you're the one who can break it. But the truth is, Lyra, you can't break it. Not without destroying everything."

A chill ran down her spine as the realization hit her. The man she had been drawn to, the man who had awakened something deep inside her, was not a savior. He was a force that would either save or destroy them all.

And Lyra was caught in the middle, unable to escape the storm that was closing in around her.

Nine

Torn by Fate

The air in the mansion was suffocating, thick with secrets that pressed in from all sides. Lyra's footsteps echoed as she walked through the dimly lit halls, each footfall growing heavier as if the weight of her father's words had turned the very ground beneath her into lead. She had never felt so disconnected from the world around her, so distanced from everything she had once known. The walls of the estate, once a sanctuary, now felt like a prison—a place where lies tangled with truth, and every corner seemed to hide a piece of the puzzle she could never quite solve.

Her father's confession still rang in her ears. You are the key. His words had torn through her, leaving her reeling, her heart pounding with the realization of how little she truly understood about her bloodline, about herself. Control the curse, or it consumes us all. The truth of it, so simple and yet so horrifying, wrapped around her like a noose, and no matter how much she tried to breathe, it squeezed tighter with every thought.

But it wasn't just the curse. It wasn't just the bloodline, the legacy of darkness that had shaped everything about her family. It was Caden.

Caden, who had walked into her life like a storm, bringing with him both the promise of freedom and the danger of destruction. His presence had awakened something deep inside her—a desire, a longing she couldn't ignore. His touch had branded her, marking her as something more than just the girl she had once been. Every time he was near, the world seemed to shift beneath her feet, and every time their gazes met, she was pulled deeper into the web of his words, his promises, his lies.

She had tried to resist him. She had tried to keep her distance, to hold onto the pieces of herself that weren't entangled in his shadows. But every time she thought she had made sense of it, every time she thought she could push him away, she found herself drawn back to him—his voice, his touch, the intensity in his eyes that made her feel like she was standing on the edge of a precipice, ready to fall.

Tonight, she couldn't escape it. She couldn't escape him.

Lyra found herself at the edge of the garden, the path winding through the overgrown hedges like a dark river, leading her into the depths of the estate's grounds. The moon was high in the sky, its pale light casting long shadows on the ground, and the air was heavy with the scent of wet earth and the faint whisper of leaves stirring in the wind. It was a quiet night, but Lyra could feel the storm inside her, the turbulence that had been building ever since Caden had walked into her life.

She didn't know where she was going, only that she needed to be alone, away from everything. Away from her father's warnings, away from the curse, away from the decision that was looming over her like a stormcloud she couldn't outrun.

And then, as if the world itself had been waiting for her to step into it, she saw him.

Caden stood at the far end of the garden, just beyond the circle of moonlight, his silhouette sharp against the darkness. The sight of him sent a jolt through her chest, and her breath caught in her throat. He was always like this—always in the shadows, always lurking just out of reach. But tonight, there was something different about him, something that made her heart race even faster. His posture was tense, as though he had been waiting for her, and when his eyes met hers, she felt that familiar pull—the magnetic force that seemed to draw her to him, against her will.

He didn't speak at first, his gaze holding hers with an intensity that made it impossible for her to look away. The air between them was charged, thick with everything they had never said, with everything they had never dared to admit.

"Lyra," Caden finally said, his voice low, rough, as if he were fighting to control something deep inside himself. "You've been avoiding me."

"I'm not avoiding you," Lyra replied, though the words felt like a lie the moment they left her lips. She wasn't just avoiding him—she was avoiding the truth. Avoiding the pull that he had on her, the way he made her feel as if she were standing on the edge of something dangerous, something she wasn't sure she wanted to fall into.

"Then what is this?" Caden stepped forward, his boots crunching on the gravel, closing the space between them until they were standing so close that Lyra could feel the heat of his body, the faint scent of his cologne mixing with the damp earth around them. "What is it you're running from, Lyra? What's really stopping you from coming to me?"

His words hit her like a punch to the gut, and she took a step back, the weight of them settling over her like a dark cloud. "I'm not running from anything," she said, though the words were hollow, empty. "I'm trying to figure out what's real. What's the truth."

Caden's eyes softened, and for the briefest moment, she saw something in them—something that wasn't just desire, wasn't just the burning intensity that had always been there. There was something else, something more vulnerable, more fragile.

"You think you can control this," he said quietly, his voice barely above a whisper. "But you can't. You can't control what's happening to you, what's happening to us."

The words sank in, slow and deliberate, like stones thrown into the still waters of her mind. She had known this, on some level. She had known that whatever this was between them, whatever pull Caden had on her, was beyond her control. It was something older, something darker than either of them could fully understand.

But it wasn't just that. It wasn't just the curse that loomed over them like an unspoken truth. It was the way she felt when he was near—like the world shifted, like everything else faded into the background, leaving only the two of them, tangled in the space between them.

Lyra took a deep breath, her hands shaking as she reached for the edge of the stone bench nearby. She needed to steady herself, needed to ground herself in the reality she had been trying to escape. But there was no escaping him. There was no escaping the pull, the desire, the fear.

"What do you want from me?" she asked, her voice barely above a whisper, as if speaking any louder would shatter the fragile hold she had on herself.

Caden's gaze was intense as he stepped even closer, his body nearly touching hers now. She could feel his breath against her cheek, warm and steady, as if he were trying to steady her, as if he were trying to anchor her to something real.

"I want you to understand," he said softly, his voice a mix of tenderness and something darker, something more urgent. "I want you to understand that you're not just the girl you think you are. You are part of something much bigger, something that neither of us can escape. But I'm here. And I'll stay with you, no matter what happens. No matter what choice you make."

Lyra felt the weight of his words settle over her like a blanket, suffocating and comforting all at once. She wanted to believe him. She wanted to trust him. But she didn't know if she could.

"Do you think I'm ready for this?" she asked, her voice breaking, the question coming out as a raw plea. "Do you think I'm ready for what's coming?"

Caden's eyes darkened, his hand reaching out to gently touch her face, his fingers brushing against her cheek with a tenderness that took her breath away. "No," he whispered. "I don't think you're ready. But you're already in it, Lyra. And there's no turning back now."

The world seemed to tilt as he leaned in, his lips brushing against hers in a kiss that was both gentle and fierce, a kiss that promised everything and nothing at once. Lyra's body responded before her mind could catch up, her arms wrapping around him as she lost herself in the moment. But even as she kissed him, even as the world around her faded away, she knew—deep down—that she was standing at the edge of something she couldn't control, something that would change everything.

And when the kiss finally broke, when they pulled apart, their foreheads resting together in the soft glow of the moonlight, Lyra knew that no matter how hard she tried to fight it, no matter how much she wanted to deny it, she was already lost.

Ten

The Final Stand

The night had grown oppressive, a thick weight pressing down on the world outside. Lyra stood at the window, her hands resting lightly on the cold glass, as the storm raged against the estate. The wind howled, and the trees outside swayed with a violence that mirrored the turmoil inside her chest. Every gust of wind sent a chill through her, and though the temperature in the room was warm, the cold seemed to settle deep into her bones.

She couldn't shake the feeling that something was about to break. It had been building for days—weeks, really—and now the tension had reached its peak. The warnings, the threats, her father's words, and Caden's promises had all woven together into a tangled mess of uncertainty and fear. The decision she had been avoiding had come, and it was standing right before her.

The choice.

Her bloodline. The curse. Caden. All of it had led her to this moment, a precipice she couldn't avoid any longer.

She thought about Caden—his intense gaze, the way his lips felt against hers, the quiet but insistent pull that had drawn her to him. His words echoed in her mind, You can't fight this. The truth. The truth that had become a storm within her, swirling in ways she could no longer ignore.

Suddenly, a knock at the door broke through her thoughts. Her heart leapt in her chest, the unexpected sound sending a shiver down her spine.

"Lyra?" The voice on the other side of the door was soft but filled with an undeniable urgency. Caden.

Her pulse quickened as she moved to the door, every step heavier than the last. She opened it to find him standing there, his dark eyes scanning her with a mixture of concern and something else—something far darker that seemed to linger just beneath the surface.

"You're not safe here," Caden said before she could say a word, his voice rough, laced with a sharp edge of worry. "They know you're here. We don't have much time."

Her breath caught in her throat. "Who knows?" Her mind raced, every possible scenario flashing through her mind. Her father's warnings, the whispered threats, the looming presence of the curse—it all felt like it was closing in around her.

"Everyone," he said grimly, stepping inside the room without waiting for an invitation. "They've been watching you. They know what you are, and they know what you can do. They won't stop until they have you."

Lyra took a step back, her mind spinning as she tried to make sense of what he was saying. She had always known there were dangers surrounding her, but this? This felt different. There was an intensity to Caden's words, a weight that made her stomach twist with a familiar, sharp fear.

"What are we supposed to do?" she whispered, her voice barely audible against the storm outside.

He closed the door behind him, his back to her, the muscles in his shoulders tight. He didn't answer right away, and in that silence, Lyra could feel the storm building between them, the weight of unspoken truths, of decisions that had already been made. The tension was palpable, crackling in the air like static before a thunderstorm.

"We fight," Caden said at last, turning to face her. "We do this now, or it will be too late. You can't run from this anymore. It's here. It's always been here."

She looked up at him, and in that moment, everything around her fell away—the storm, the mansion, the years of uncertainty. It was just the two of them. The pull she had tried to resist, the bond between them that had only deepened, surged like an undercurrent. There was no going back.

"What do you mean?" Lyra asked, her voice low, barely above a whisper.

His gaze softened for just a moment, but there was no warmth in his eyes, only an aching truth. "You're the key, Lyra. You always have been. But now… now it's your choice. If you want to save us all, you have to make a decision. You can either give in, let them control you, or you can fight. But if you fight, it'll cost you everything."

Her heart thundered in her chest. It'll cost you everything. The words hit her like a physical blow. She had already given so much—her life, her peace, her heart—and now, Caden was telling her she would have to give more. She felt the weight of it pressing down on her, her chest tightening with the heaviness of the decision she had been avoiding.

"Everything?" Lyra repeated, her voice shaky. "What do you mean?"

Caden took a step closer to her, his eyes never leaving hers, as if he were trying to anchor her to the present moment, to the reality that was unfolding between them. "The curse isn't just something that's been placed on you, Lyra. It's inside of you. It's been inside of you all along. And when it comes to a head, when it breaks free… you'll either control it, or it will control you."

The words felt like they were suffocating her. The room spun slightly, her vision narrowing as the weight of his statement settled over her like a fog. She had always known there was more to her bloodline, more to her than she could ever truly understand, but hearing it like this… Hearing it from Caden, whose words seemed to rip apart every layer of the truth she had built around herself, made it real.

"This is bigger than you and me, Lyra," Caden continued, his voice low, but with a sharp edge to it. "This is about survival. Your survival. Our survival."

Her heart pounded in her chest, the urgency in his words clawing at her, pulling her toward something she wasn't sure she was ready for. The world outside raged against the walls of the mansion, the storm growing louder as if it were reflecting the chaos inside of her. She felt the tug of something ancient, something powerful, and she wasn't sure she was ready to face it, let alone wield it.

"You don't have to do this," Caden whispered, as though reading her mind. "You can still walk away. We can run, we can disappear."

Lyra's hands trembled at her sides, her mind a whirlwind of thoughts, of emotions too tangled to unravel. Part of her wanted to run, to take Caden's offer and disappear, to leave behind everything that had ever held her back. But another part of her—the part that had always known there was something bigger, something darker—was screaming at her to stay, to face whatever was coming.

She looked up at him, her voice shaking but steady. "What happens if I don't fight?"

Caden's face hardened, the softness from before gone, replaced with the cold resolve of someone who had already made their peace with the decision. "If you don't fight, they will control you. They will use you as a weapon, Lyra. The curse will destroy you. There's no other way."

Her heart lurched in her chest, the weight of his words heavy on her. She didn't know if she could do this. She didn't know if she was strong enough to face what was coming. But she couldn't let the fear swallow her, couldn't let it control her.

"I'm not going to let them win," Lyra said, her voice stronger now, her resolve hardening like stone. "I won't let them take me."

The air seemed to shift around them as she spoke, the tension between them crackling like an electric charge. Caden stepped closer to her, his hand reaching out to gently touch her face, his thumb brushing against her skin. The gesture was gentle, but there was an urgency behind it, a silent plea for her to understand the magnitude of what was about to happen.

"This is it, Lyra," he whispered. "We fight together. Or we don't fight at all."

For a long moment, neither of them moved. The world outside seemed to hold its breath, the storm outside echoing the storm inside her heart. Lyra looked up at Caden, seeing the fear in his eyes, but also the determination. She could feel his heartbeat, steady and sure, beneath her fingertips as she reached out to touch his chest.

And in that moment, Lyra knew what she had to do. She had to fight. She had to face the curse, face everything that had been building toward this moment. The storm, the truth, the darkness—it was all part of her now.

She wasn't afraid anymore.

Together, they would face whatever came next.

Eleven

A Love Rekindled

The darkness outside seemed endless, a vast expanse of blackness stretching toward a horizon that Lyra could not see, could not touch. The storm had passed, but the air felt thick with the aftermath—heavy, laden with the remnants of the chaos that had swept through the estate. The mansion felt empty now, hollow, as though the walls themselves were holding their breath, waiting for something to break, something to shift.

Lyra stood at the edge of the balcony once more, her hands resting on the cold stone railing as she gazed out at the world beyond. The wind had died down, but the chill remained, seeping into her skin, into her very bones. She had never felt so cold, so disconnected from the warmth of her own life. Everything had changed in the span of a few short days, and she wasn't sure she recognized the world around her anymore.

The pull of the curse, the bloodline that had always been a part of her, was undeniable now. There was no escaping it, no running from it. And there was no escaping him—Caden.

The thought of him, of the way he had looked at her, of the intensity in his eyes when he spoke of the fight ahead, made her chest tighten. His presence, his touch, had awakened something deep inside her, something that was both exhilarating and terrifying. She had tried to deny it, to ignore it, but now… now, there was no turning back.

She closed her eyes, her mind racing with the weight of everything she had learned, everything she had felt. The storm had passed, but the storm inside her heart was just beginning. The decision to fight, to embrace the curse or to let it consume her, was no longer a distant thought. It was now. The path ahead was unclear, the cost of the fight unknown, but one thing was certain—there was no going back.

A soft creak of the door behind her made her stiffen. She didn't need to turn around to know who it was. The heat of his presence, the steady rhythm of his breath, told her everything she needed to know. Caden.

She could feel him before he even spoke, the air around them thick with the tension that always seemed to linger between them. It was as if the space between them crackled, charged with an energy she couldn't escape.

"You've been quiet," Caden said, his voice low, steady, as he stepped closer, his boots soft against the marble floor. "Too quiet."

Lyra didn't turn to face him, didn't need to. She could feel his gaze on her, piercing through the quiet, and it made her heart race faster. She wasn't ready to look at him yet—not with everything still swirling inside her, not with the weight of their last conversation hanging heavy in the air.

"I don't know what I'm supposed to do," Lyra said finally, her voice hoarse, as though the words had been caught in her throat for far too long. "I don't know if I'm strong enough to make the choice. I don't know if I'm strong enough to fight."

The silence between them stretched, thick and palpable. She could feel his presence drawing closer, could hear the soft shift of his clothing as he moved.

"You're stronger than you know," Caden murmured, his voice softer now, almost tender, as if the weight of her words had struck him in ways she couldn't fully understand. "You've always been stronger. You just don't see it yet. You've been fighting this fight your whole life, Lyra. But now… now, you have the chance to finish it. To take control of everything that's been controlling you."

She closed her eyes again, his words settling over her like a weight she couldn't shake. She wanted to believe him. She wanted to believe that she could stand up to the curse, that she could fight and win, but the fear that had always lived at the edges of her mind was growing louder, more insistent. What if she couldn't control it? What if it consumed her like it had consumed so many before her?

"You don't have to do this alone," Caden continued, his voice softening, and when Lyra finally turned to face him, she saw that his eyes—those dark, storm-filled eyes—were filled with something else. Something deeper, something more vulnerable than she had ever seen before. "I'll be with you. No matter what happens."

His words pierced through the walls she had built around herself, and before she could stop it, her heart seemed to leap in her chest. There was something in the way he looked at her, something that made everything inside her ache, that made everything she had ever known feel insignificant.

"I don't know how to trust this," she whispered, her voice barely audible, her throat tight. "I don't know how to trust you."

Caden didn't pull away, didn't retreat, though he must have felt the distance between them, the invisible wall she had constructed. Instead, he stepped closer, his presence overwhelming, and he reached out, gently cupping her face in his hands, his thumbs brushing softly across her skin.

"You don't have to trust me," he said, his voice hushed, a faint tremor in his words that made her heart tighten. "But you have to trust yourself. You have to trust what's inside you."

His thumb brushed against her lips, and Lyra shuddered at the soft, intimate contact, her heart thudding in her chest. She didn't want this. She didn't want to feel this. But it was already too late. She had already given herself to him in ways she couldn't explain, in ways that had nothing to do with the curse, with the fight. It was something deeper, something more primal, and she couldn't escape it.

She reached up, her hands trembling as she placed them over his, feeling the warmth of his touch, the steady beat of his pulse beneath her fingertips. For a moment, neither of them spoke. They stood there, facing each other, caught in the quiet, in the space between them that neither of them knew how to bridge.

And then, as if the world outside had finally given way to the storm inside her, she leaned forward, closing the distance between them, her lips brushing against his in a kiss that was both hesitant and fierce. The world tilted on its axis as she kissed him, her body responding to him in ways she had no control over, no explanation for. There was nothing gentle about the kiss. It was raw, filled with everything they had never said, with everything they had never dared to admit.

When they finally broke apart, breathless, her chest rising and falling in quick, shallow breaths, Lyra felt as though the world had shifted beneath her. She felt it in her very soul, the way his presence had filled the space, the way their connection had deepened with every touch, every kiss. The weight of the choice still hung between them, but for the first time in days, she didn't feel so lost.

"Lyra," Caden whispered, his voice a low rumble against her skin. "We fight. Together. Or we don't fight at all."

She looked up at him then, her hands still resting on his chest, and in that moment, she understood. She understood that there was no turning back, no walking away from the storm that was coming. There was no running from the curse, from the choices that lay ahead. There was only the fight.

And with that understanding, she made her decision.

"I'm with you," she said softly, her voice steady now, her heart filled with a resolve she hadn't known she was capable of. "We fight. Together."

And for the first time in what felt like forever, she allowed herself to believe it.

Twelve

Under the Crimson Moon

⁓❦⁓

The night was alive with the hum of the earth beneath Lyra's feet, the pulse of something ancient, something powerful. The estate, so familiar just days before, now felt like a place she had never known, a place she could never return to. She stood at the edge of the garden, her breath coming in shallow bursts as she looked up at the crimson moon. It hung low in the sky, its deep red light casting an eerie glow over everything, turning the familiar landscape into something unrecognizable. The air was thick with the promise of change, a reckoning that could not be avoided.

Caden stood beside her, his presence like a shadow wrapped around her, both comforting and unsettling. He had been by her side through it all—the whispered warnings, the sleepless nights, the weight of the curse that had bound her to this moment. His touch had always been a silent promise, but now, with the moon casting its blood-red glow on them, that promise felt heavier than ever.

"I thought this was just a myth," Lyra whispered, her voice trembling despite herself as she glanced at the moon again. "A story. A curse that's been passed down through my bloodline."

Caden's gaze was fixed on the horizon, his jaw tight as he watched the wind whip through the trees, bending them with an eerie force. The tension in the air mirrored the storm inside him, and Lyra could feel it radiating from him, a magnetic force that only pulled her closer.

"It's not a myth," he said quietly, his voice low, almost reverent. "It's real. And it's been waiting for you, Lyra. Waiting for this moment."

Lyra turned to him, her heart pounding in her chest. "What do you mean? What happens now?"

His eyes met hers, the darkness of his gaze swallowing her whole. She could see the struggle in his eyes, the conflict that had been present ever since he first stepped into her life. He reached out, his hand brushing against hers, the contact sending a surge of warmth through her, even as the chill of the night wrapped around them.

"The curse was never meant to be broken," he said, his voice hushed, as if the very words might shatter the world around them. "It's meant to control you. To control all of us. And there's only one way to stop it. Only one way to stop them."

"Them?" Lyra echoed, her pulse quickening as she leaned in closer to him. "Who are you talking about?"

Caden's jaw tightened further, the tension in his body palpable, as though he were holding something back, something dangerous. He stepped closer, his presence enveloping her, but it wasn't enough to ease the growing knot of fear in her stomach.

"The ones who have been waiting for you," he said, his voice laced with a mixture of anger and something darker, something Lyra couldn't quite place. "The ones who have been controlling your family, manipulating you from the shadows. They know what you are, and they're coming for you."

Her heart stuttered in her chest as the weight of his words settled over her like a stone. "I don't understand," she whispered. "I thought you were trying to help me. You said you would protect me. Why would you…"

"Because I'm part of it too," he interrupted, his voice fierce now, as though the truth was finally ripping its way to the surface. "I was never supposed to be the one to protect you. I was supposed to be the one to make sure the curse continues, to make sure you fulfill your role. But then you came into my life, and everything changed. You changed everything."

Lyra's breath caught in her throat as she took a step back, the distance between them growing, even as her body screamed for him to come closer. The pull she felt for him, the heat that had burned through her the moment their eyes met, was undeniable, but this—this truth—felt like a knife to the heart.

"What does that mean?" she whispered, barely able to speak the words.

Caden hesitated for a moment, his eyes flicking to the moon again before returning to her. The air between them seemed to thicken, charged with an energy that made the world around them seem still, silent.

"It means," he said slowly, each word dripping with the weight of a long-buried secret, "that we are both tied to the same destiny. The curse isn't just something that's been passed down through your bloodline. It's been passed down through mine too. And no matter how much we want to fight it, no matter how much you want to deny it, we're both part of it. Part of them."

Lyra felt the ground beneath her shift, the world tilting on its axis. Her knees felt weak, but she refused to let him see it, refused to let him see how much she was shaking inside.

"So all of this…" she began, her voice cracking as she tried to put the pieces together. "All of this was planned? You were sent here to…"

"To keep you in line," Caden finished for her, his voice almost bitter. "To make sure the curse went as it was supposed to. To make sure you never broke free."

The words hit her like a slap, and she felt the sting of betrayal, sharp and sudden, even though she knew, deep down, that she had always known.

"But something changed," Caden continued, stepping even closer now, his breath coming faster, his chest rising and falling with the weight of the words between them. "Something in you changed me. Something in me changed when I met you."

Lyra swallowed hard, her heart hammering in her chest as the truth, the full weight of it, settled over her. She had always known there was something more between them, something deeper, something that bound them together. But to know that it wasn't just fate, wasn't just the pull of destiny—it was their shared curse, their shared bond, that had led them here… it made everything feel even more impossible.

"I don't know what to do," she whispered, her voice barely audible, the words barely escaping her lips as the weight of the decision ahead crushed down on her. "I don't know how to stop this. How to fight them."

Caden reached for her then, his hands gentle as they cupped her face, his thumb brushing across her cheek with a tenderness that seemed out of place in the midst of everything they were facing.

"You don't have to fight alone, Lyra," he said softly, his voice barely above a whisper, as though the very act of speaking the words might break something fragile. "You never have to fight alone. I'm with you. Always."

His lips brushed against hers in a kiss that was soft, almost tentative at first, but it deepened with the urgency of their situation, with the realization that everything they had fought for, everything they had been through, had led them to this moment.

The kiss wasn't just a promise of love—it was a promise of something deeper, something more powerful. It was a promise of rebellion against the fate that had been written for them, of standing together in the face of everything that sought to tear them apart.

As they pulled away, breathless, Lyra looked up at him, her chest rising and falling with each heavy breath. The moon above them seemed to glow brighter now, its crimson light bathing them both in its eerie glow, casting long shadows across the garden. She felt the weight of it—the weight of the decision, the weight of their shared curse, the weight of the war they were about to fight.

"I'm with you," she said, her voice steady now, her heart filled with something more than just fear. "I'll fight. I'll fight with you."

Caden's eyes softened, and for the briefest moment, he allowed himself to show her the vulnerability that had been buried beneath his guarded exterior. "Then let's finish this," he said, his voice low, full of determination. "Together."

And under the crimson moon, Lyra knew, with every fiber of her being, that there was no turning back. They were in this together, and whatever came next, they would face it side by side.